75 *Golden Years*

Edited by

Andrew Head

First published in Great Britain in 1998 by
POETRY NOW
1-2 Wainman Road, Woodston,
Peterborough, PE2 7BU
Telephone (01733) 230746
Fax (01733) 230751

Copyright Contributors 1998

HB ISBN 0 75430 466 3
SB ISBN 0 75430 467 1

FOREWORD

Although we are a nation of poetry writers we are accused of not reading poetry and not buying poetry books: after many years of listening to the incessant gripes of poetry publishers, I can only assume that the books they publish, in general, are books that most people do not want to read.

Poetry should not be obscure, introverted, and as cryptic as a crossword puzzle: it is the poet's duty to reach out and embrace the world.

The world owes the poet nothing and we should not be expected to dig and delve into a rambling discourse searching for some inner meaning.

The reason we write poetry (and almost all of us do) is because we want to communicate: an ideal; an idea; or a specific feeling. Poetry is as essential in communication, as a letter; a radio; a telephone, and the main criteria for selecting the poems in this anthology is very simple: they communicate.

On the 23rd April, 75 years ago, Wembley Stadium staged its first sporting spectacular: the FA Cup Final between Bolton Wanderers and West Ham United.

This collection of poems is to celebrate that momentous occasion. Expressing the poet's feelings and emotions when their favourite team scores that all important goal.

75 Golden Years is an inspirational book of verse with an insight into today's modern football supporter.

CONTENTS

HOWAY THE LADS!

(Apologies to G K Chesterton)

Before the Spartans came to Blyth, or Magpies were full grow'd,
The little Geordie drunkard made the famous Scotswood Road.
A rambling road, a shambling road, that wanders up and down
And after him the polis ran, the bailiff, half the town.
A busy road, a boozy road, where we did drink our fill
The night we went to Gallowgate - by way of Rowlands Gill.

I have no truck with bailiffs, I've never thumped a copper,
And if I took on half the town I'd come a right old cropper.
But I would bash their heids in if they came all array'd
To straighten out the crooked road the drunken Geordie made.
Where you would see wor lad and me, with broon ale in our hands
The night we went to James' Park - by way of Tynemouth sands.

His sins were all forgiven him, or why do boozers thrive
To gan alang the Scotswood Road, like when he was alive?
He staggered forth from left to right and knew not which was which
But the Blue Star shone above him when they found him in the ditch.
So glare at us, or swear at us, we did not see so clear
The night we went to Roker Park - by way of South Shields pier.

My friends, we may not go again to see the Blaydon Races
And all the lads and lasses with their bright and smiling faces
But I will walk beside you to St James' Leazes end
And we will shout 'Howay the lads, Newcassel's won agen!'
For there are cup ties to be played, and finals to be seen
Before we go to Paradise - by way of Jesmond Dene.

E Barnett

SNAPSHOT

You could break it all down to its constituent parts
To mechanics and geometry
Fulcrums and trigonometry
The whole thing an equation of power, speed and time
Forces at angles
Points on a line.

But what I recall is a bubble in time,
Something rounded and smooth like a stone from the shore,
Where all movement was fluid and
The ball curved in the air.

A snapshot of perfection, a glimpse of the sublime.

The mid-fielder ran parallel to the halfway line
The turned á la Cruyff
Glanced up
Leaned back
And let go with his left
A 25 yard pass
A rainbow in white
Arching a path over forward and back
It bounced once and then on its way down
The forward's left foot volleyed it hard
Hard towards the goal from some 20 yards
And as it seemed to dip under the bar
The keeper in a private arc of his own
Curled back at the last
And tipped it off course
Then fell back to earth
Back to sand and wet grass.

In this gallery of art, I had just witnessed class
And there are some who say football's just a kick in the grass.

Kevin McNamara

FOOTBALL CRAZY

Years ago, our three kids, were mad about the game,
Football I mean, but nowadays it's really not the same.
A flask of coffee, to be shared, with Dad and Auntie Chris,
A sandwich each to chomp on, they really thought it bliss.
Cheering their heroes till they were hoarse,
Elated when they won,
But the cost of admission these days
Is spoiling all the fun.
How can a chap in this day and age,
With sons, and even daughters,
Afford to take them to every match,
They'd very soon be paupers.
Especially as the kids want kits,
And as these change so often,
They too expect to change them, so
It really costs a fortune.
If the players weren't paid such a fabulous wage,
And those at the top got less,
Then maybe the admission fees
Could be reduced I guess.
Then the working man would be able to go
With his family more, not less.

Olive Smith

YESTERDAY, ONCE MORE

One moment in time
Frozen from your mind -
'Ten against eleven!'
The crowd roars!
The spirit soars!
Whiteside scores!
And the Cup is yours
Total recall - total heaven.

G J Ball

WEMBLEY WOUNDS

I regrettably hear that dreaded sound
A whistle pierces the air around
Exhausted bodies fall to the ground
Unbearable disappointment, to the third division we are bound

Tears from my soul are bled
As I look at the turf the players have for a bed
Consoling people gently tread
Among the sweat where morale is dead

The chests expand gasping for breath
As on a battlefield the losers resigned to death
The cameras divert to the lifting of the cup
The losers are left to pick themselves back up

Wembley is no place to lose
Promotion via the play-offs I would never choose
It's an agonising ride of unbearable strain
For three quarters of the applicants the result is pain

The swift journey up on a summer's day
Contrasts the monotonous return, the world bathed in grey
Cheerful excited pre-match chat
Changes to silence, everyone in their own thoughts sat.

Stephen Ware

UNTITLED

Sometimes I'm a spectator
There's so little I can do
I can be there for the winners
And support the losers too

When goals are very far apart
And life at its worst for me
I seem to be stuck in there alone
Support a team-mate's all unknown

But when I take my place
And I play both fair and square
I have the love of all the earth
And my victories I can share

I've played so many matches
Both home games and away
Some rougher and tougher than others
But loyalty and support helps me stay

So I mustn't be disheartened
Life is but a football match
There's as much fun in the passes
As there is in every catch

My colleagues make it easy
Our team's motto is not news
'It's the taking part that matters
Not if we win or lose.'

So when my game is over
Whether goals are scored or not
I know I'll be a winner
If I gave life my best shot.

Yvonne McGrath

THE PLIGHT OF CARDIFF CITY

It was the month of May in 27,
When the bluebirds won the cup.
The marble halls of Highbury,
Said their goalie messed it up.
The Arsenal lad in goal that day,
Was Welsh and kept his pride.
He said the ball had spun from him
And hit him on the side.
But after that the Arsenal boss
Said pack your bags and ride
Those glory days of 27
Have yet to be repeated.
We play the likes of Barnet now
And often get defeated.
There's talk of a big sponsor
Who wants to move our ground
He promised that in three years' time,
We will be premier bound.
But then I stop and think a while
And say 'I've heard it all before,'
Please can someone come and help us
Or we'll be here no more.
Now here's a small reminder
Of the Bluebirds' fans today,
Our attendances so poor,
Because supporters stay away.
But if we had a winning team,
They'd come back in their thousands
And give the people of South Wales
A team they were once proud of.

Kerry Richards

KING ERIC

Football is a most beautiful game
But so many players are all the same
Team after team they're just like clones
But a few shine bright like Vinnie Jones

There's the old ones like Pelé George Best and Platini
And now there's Ravanelli Bergkamp and Paolo Maldini

So who's up next from my football tombolla
There's not many that compare to David Ginola

And now that the end is drawing nearer
I mustn't forget the great Alan Shearer

So who is the best it'll be a real fight
Will it be Del Piero Paul Ince or Ian Wright

But by far the brightest shining star
Has got to be Eric Cantona

With such flair speed and outright skill
He leaves the others standing still

What more can be said but just one thing
That Eric the Red is the king of kings.

René Bacquain

FA CUP

'Why don't you score?' the fans always scream
If we win this it would be a dream
If we lose I'll be extremely fed up
Please let us win the FA cup.'

'Look at that ref, how can you allow
That player to commit such an awful foul?
Bring on the stretcher, he can't get up
Now we'll never win the FA Cup.'

'Pass the ball! God bless my soul
He's kicked it in the top of the goal
They've done it. Things are looking up
We've finally won the FA Cup.'

'What a sight for the world to see
The boys shaking the hands of Royalty
The captain lifts the thing right up
The thing that is the FA Cup.'

Sebastian Horan (13)

ALL IN THE GAME

Luscious green and chalk white,
Kaleidoscope colours of fans,
Bobble hats, rattles and programmes,
It's all in the game, my friends.

Chanting, cheering and clapping,
Emotions forever changing,
Friendship, passion and loyalty,
It's all in the game, my friends.

Physical fitness and talent,
FA Cup drama and glory,
Worldwide support and enjoyment,
It's all in the game, my friends.

Bergkamp, Pele and Charlton,
Legends live on in our minds,
Savouring the beauty and wonder,
It's all in the game, my friends.

Paul Napleton

SATURDAY JOURNEY

Check my tickets, count my cash,
Grab my scarf, I have to dash
To the station; train awaits;
Happy journey, with my mates.
Will we score? - of course we will!
Probably beat them seven-nil!

Lime Street Station, just the same,
Thousands going to the game.
Laugh and joke with friends we meet,
Anticipation floods the street.
Take my seat with pounding heart;
The teams warm up, the game will start.

From the centre, to and fro,
Won a corner, here we go!
'You'll never walk alone,' we sing,
'Owen's great, but Fowler's king!'
Half time comes - but there's no score,
If we can't have seven, let's have four!

Second half: now raindrops fall;
They're slipping and sliding with the ball!
Time's nearly up, Ref, can't you see?
That should have been a penalty!
The whistle sounds, there is no more.
The teams depart. There is no score.

Hands in pockets, heads bowed low,
Dejected, gloomy, home we go.
Lime Street Station, just the same,
Thousands coming from the game.
Journey over, it's hard to speak . . .
Except for, 'See you all - next week.'

Joyce Bradley

GAS, GHOSTS AND SWEDES

It's good to look back and remember the past
But never forget there's tomorrow
And a million memories of Eastville days
Should bring happiness not sorrow
But it's eleven whole years since they pushed up the rent
And effectively brought down the curtain
And the Tote End fell silent and the Rovers moved out
And began a new chapter at Twerton
But time takes its toll and what's left of the stadium
Looks bleak and forlorn and drab
And it's hard to imagine those days of Geoff Bradford
Alfie Biggs, Jackie Pitt, Smash 'n' Grab
When Petherbridge, Jarman and Roost ruled the roost
And yes, Messrs Holloway and Kite
But then all good things finally come to an end
And Eastville said 'Irene Goodnight'
And now all that is found
At our beloved old ground
Are the doggies that run
Around and around
So take one last trip down to Eastville and see
A shadow of the stadium, it once used to be
Put it out of its misery, let it suffer no more
And build a jumped up Scandinavian furniture store.

Jon Cursiter

THE FEARS OF RELEGATION

Football, football everywhere,
No other sport can compare,
The crowd's live and electric, everyone's cheering,
It's like winning the league, the cup or even going up,
There is no better feeling.

The team I support are red and white,
And there really is no better sight,
Your top striker goes down injured, he's out for the rest
of the season,
Could there really be another reason?

May is here,
There are relegation fears,
Are we staying up or going down?
We'll never know until the times comes around.

The time has come,
it looks like we won,
There is no relegation,
Tonight I'm sure there will be a big celebration.

It gives you stress,
But it is the best,
Football, football everywhere,
No other sport can compare.

Sarah Gray

FRANCE '98

France '98 was worth its weight
In Golden Goals, Mercedes and Rolls Royceing
Rejoicing: street-urchins knee-deep in ticker-tape
A Presidential order for all Brazilians to celebrate . . .
Blown asunder by cruel fate
As no! Alas! A crucial blow: Ronaldo has stubbed his toe
From the slums of St Paulo and Rio de Janeiro
Hark at the sighs, the cries, the wails of woe
And with bikini'd Brazilian spirits low
With storm clouds gathering in their skies
The Moroccans delight and surprise and the Norwegians capitalise
A late winner from Tore Andre Flo kills off the dream of two in a row

Bill Shankly is taken literally and Zagallo is taken critically
But neither Spain nor Italy will hold aloft the Jules Rimet
The Latinos react bitterly, mass shootings up in Sicily
But in New York there's only apathy, it's just another day
Until that is, and with the Americans saluting the flag to a man
Before the final against Iran
Saddam Hussein enters the fray
Jolting Clinton from his 3 o'clock lay, to hiss:
'Your men showed us the way in Hanoi
Now down on your knees and pray, boy
This time you will inhale, so enjoy'
And then he unleashes his evil plan
Nuking Paris, Washington and Tehran
Doing a lap of honour, and blowing the crowd a kiss
But crediting all his glory to the Koran, nice man that he is

And that's the story of France '98
Saddam at last getting his revenge for Kuwait.

Phil Klein

ENGLAND MY ENGLAND

I meet up with the boys,
a motley crew one and all
The buzz is everywhere,
down the pub and up Wembley Way
The nation's best will soon perform,
challenging another foreign foe

Into the pub we venture,
to be met by yet more national pride
Pint after pint slips down,
the vocal chords well lubricated
We'll need all our strength and passion,
to urge the boys on to victory

Into our gladiators' arena we enter,
always amazed by the sacred temple
The anticipation and expectation grows,
draining even the most stout of men
We stand to attention hand on heart,
singing our anthem for all we're worth

Our warriors salute us with clenched fists,
as they ready themselves to do battle
The whistle goes and the crowd roars,
urging our heroes to deliver the goods
The opposition perplexed and in disarray,
have no answer to the constant barrage

Our battle-scared soldiers in white,
have seen off yet another enemy
We're all in seventh heaven,
delirious, ecstatic and proud
Our dreary lives are worth living,
as dreams become reality once more.

Alex Alexandrou

Boro's Season '96–'97

We'd won lots of matches
We were on a high
then the FA came along
and squashed us like a fly.

Why don't they like us?
because they have southern roots
they snatched away all our glory
those grey men in grey suits.

When we wanted to postpone the match
the FA said there'd be no trouble
but then they took away three points
that really burst our bubble.

Juninho tried to save us
single-handedly
but his brilliant efforts were a failure
without the deducted three.

Everyone was sad on the last day at Leeds
to see Juninho cry
the FA made it hard for him
but I know he really did try.

But when I look back at last season
I should not feel pain
'Boro have a whole new season to look forward to
full of glory, winning and gain.

For such a wrongful season
I hope all the FA get the sack
as for my team do not worry
Boro will be back!

Adam Blacklock (14)

WALK ON
(Dedicated to those fans who lost their lives in the Hillsborough Tragedy on April 15th 1989)

Many fans had gone that day,
To see the Reds go Wembley way.
But none could see what lay ahead,
for 96 would soon be dead.
At 3.06 it all began,
A nightmare now for every fan.
Friends and neighbours fight for life,
A brother, sister or someone's wife.
Help was coming from all around,
As injured people lay on the ground.
Over the fences they did climb,
As people's lives were on the line.
Shouts and screams of get me free,
Another fan, another plea.
News now sent the country wide,
Another tragedy for Merseyside.
As we listen in disbelief,
Another Hysel, another grief.
Over the weeks the stories unfold,
Who's to blame we must be told.
Anfield's ground now a carpet of red,
As tributes are laid for the 96 dead.
A minute's silence in respect,
But in our thoughts what is next.
No more losses we hope and pray,
Take a note of the toll this day.
Sadness is with us, the pain's not gone,
But in Liverpool still, we will walk on.

Jamie Williams

PRELIMINARY ROUND (A CHANCE TO DREAM)

Young heart,
Young semi-pro.
First game, boots on, nerves bite, let's go.
Anticipation heightened by excited chatter
About the only cup that matters.
A chance of glory,
Maybe of instant fame?
To score the goal that might give him a game
Against a giant from division three,
And after that, who knows?
He, too, can dream of Wembley.

Tired legs,
Old pro.
He once played in a final.
Don't you know
He scored that goal that took them through,
The year that they beat Arsenal, Barnsley, Doncaster and Crewe.
And now, although he's seen it all before,
The cup gives him the chance
To relive all the thrills once more,
And dream this game in the preliminary,
Is the one he played that time at Wembley.

Stephen Ive

HOOKED ON FOOTBALL

Come and watch this game with me,
Come and sit upon my knee
And, as the kick-off commenced
I thought, I must have more sense
Than sit here, watching men play ball,
When all the ironing's in the hall.

But once the match had livened up,
And the commentator mentioned cup,
I thought of a nice cup of tea,
Whilst sitting on my husband's knee.
But I was so engrossed in game,
Football will never be the same.

And now I'm hooked on Saturday
Watching games, home and away.
I'm learning what it's all about,
'Where's my tea,' my husband shouts.
There lies the ironing in the hall,
I've got my feet up, watching football.

Daphne Dawkins

1960-1961

It had never been
done this Century
and everyone said
It would never be
Then along came
Spurs and Bill Nicholson
sweeping all before them
and The Double was won
There was Danny Boy
and Dave McKay
full of skill and
never say die
Chessboard moves
played off the cuff
this was a team playing
the game they loved
so perfection reigned at
White Hart Lane
a style of football
never to be seen again
Glory Glory Hallelujah
echoes in our ears
as we raise our glasses
to those Golden Years.

John Simons

THE WEMBLEY STORY

It all began at Wembley in the year of '23,
The Trotters and the Hammers were a joy for all to see.
Jack scored for Bolton Wanderers who garnered all the spoils,
But the policeman and his white horse won the day for all their toils.

The Gunners came in '27 and took on Cardiff City,
Their keeper Danny Lewis made a boob, 'twas such a pity.
Because of that the Welshmen won and took the Cup back home,
The one and only time the Cup to Wales did ever roam.

Matt Busby came in '34 and brought big Frank Swift too,
The referee was Stanley Rous and he his whistle blew.
The scene was too much for young Frank and when full time
                                        was sounded
Beneath his crossbar he collapsed, by colleagues was surrounded.

The fifties brought The Geordies and 'The Blaydon Races' too,
With Jackie Milburn in the van, 'twas he who scored a few.
They beat the mighty Blackpool with San Matthews in their side,
Joe Harvey trod the Royal steps to raise the cup with pride.

The sixties favoured Tottenham the double to achieve,
It was their hero Bobby Smith the siege he did relieve.
The man in Leicester's goal that day was mighty Gordon Banks,
But he could not prevent The Spurs from raiding down the flanks.

The Seventies saw Liverpool, Shanks and the boot-room boys,
And when Kev Keegan scored a brace the Kop choir raised some noise.
Poor Newcastle were shattered, Mal McDonald and Tudor,
They won the pre Cup battle but lost the Final War.

The Eighties featured Man Utd, winners twice for them,
With skipper Bryan Robson their brave captain at the helm.
The Nineties had their moments too with Cantona a star,
The fastest goal, Mark Hughes 5th tie, brought records up to par.

Don O'Doherty

THE TRUE BLUES LAMENT
(Dedicated to the Maine Rd King)

Franny don't stay away too long
We know they chanted their bitter song
But we the true, the battling blue
Supporters knew your love was true
Franny you gave us many happy years
And in the 70s even lots of cheers
Those young ones they will never know
The Francis Lee who stole the show
You never gave up you always tried
You battled hard some say you dived
'The Penalty King' you were crowned
You hammered them past as the goalies frowned
You were proud to put on that England shirt
You played so well you dished up some dirt
Then one day you came back to us in the chairman's role
The young ones expected miracles they did not see your goal
Week in and week out you sat up in your box
We needed just to see your face it looked so full of knocks
But you kept on coming back for more hoping the curse would end
The fans were cruel they chanted and some went round the bend
Many a wet Saturday we'd see you return
Hoping that one day these young players and fans would learn
You could have been at the races drinking Champagne with money
                                                        on the tote
Watching your own horses they must have had more hope
But no you chose to take the stick and then you had to go
We hope you can forgive the young for they could never know
We just hope you're not bitter now, we know your heart won't leave
Maine Road is your second home and you are not to grieve
One day you'll be welcomed back I'm sure with open arms
And one day the young blue fans will remember you for your charms
You were loyal and true there was no better blue
There was only one king it was you.

Catherine Anne Martland

WINNING THE FA CUP

When I was young
   I'd sit and dream,
Of playing for
   some football team.
My ambition then
   was only one aim,
to reach the final
   after winning each game.
To be like Keegan, Dalglish
   and the rest,
Names like Lineker
   that were simply the best.
Oh how I wanted
   to play just the same,
And hear my praises
   plus get all the fame.
But sadly for me
   when I grew up,
I knew that I'd never
   win the FA Cup.
My hopes of stardom
   were just in my dreams,
As I never got picked
   for those football teams.
You see, if only my legs
   had been more able,
I might have been one
   to put them top of the table.
So now instead
   they just get my cheer,
As I continue to follow them
   year after year.

Maureen Burns

NAKED EMOTIONS

From the throats of the excited throng
Up to the sky rose one almighty song,
The adrenaline flowed and temperatures soared
When on to the pitch the players poured.

In fast rhythm the spectators' heart-beats ran
As in earnest the game of skill began,
That elusive ball round the pitch they chased
With radar eyes that every move embraced.

With magic feet that hardly touched the ground
Round the grassy pitch the players bound,
Only one thought in their eager minds bore
To get that ball through the goals to score.

The fans, wanting the players' faults to correct
And with the right moves into their minds inject
Shouted, stamped, screamed and with no remorse
Cursed rudely until their dry throats were hoarse.

As the game carried on there suddenly appears
In brave men's eyes a sure sign of tears,
For with only five more minutes to play
Only a heavenly miracle can save the day.

The players put all their skills to the test
And for honour's sake towards victory pressed,
And the loyal fans with their nerves in a spin
Gave loud support for their team to win.

The cheering of the crowd into a crescendo grew
As into the goals that magic ball flew,
And in frenzied delight every boy and his dad
Jumped to their feet going stark raving mad.

And greater love is shown to no other
When the players hold and hug one another,
And to the golden player who saved the day
Portrayal of his heroism is put on display.

Jean M Shansky

THE FOOTBALLER

Who is lean and hungry
With those golden football shoes
My hero in the soccer world
The professional Mark Hughes

I quite like Gary Lineker
Had a yen for Emlyn Hughes
And with the Charlton brothers
I found it hard to choose

Then there's Cantona and Gascoigne
Who were not my cup of tea
And little Peter Beardsley
Who worked as well as three

But Mark Hughes has got everything
I like to see in sport
He gives his all to every game
If they lose, it's not his fault

And though he's getting on a bit
And retirement must be near
To me he is the very tops
The footballer of the year.

June Davies

GREATEST OF THEM ALL

Everyone else are the hopefuls, but I hope their hopes are dashed,
England are the underdogs, but I hope the Cup we grab.
We're long overdue another 1966,
It wasn't last year, but this time this is it.
England is made with the best from all teams,
England will become the be all and end all of all dreams.
I see France '98 as a mirror on the wall,
For it is there that we find out who is indeed, the greatest of them all.

Amanda Blades

THE DREAM THAT DID COME TRUE

Eleven men with talent
Knew they could go far
They play at Whaddon Road
Within the town of Cheltenham Spa
The players dreamed a special dream
Which for years escaped their grasp
But now this dream's become reality
To take the Cup at last.

The Cheltenham Robins are the best
They have a will that won't give in
Even if they lost a game
They still believed that they would win
The boys puff out their emblemed chests
With a great defence within their wings
They have some cracking centre forwards
That will turn them into kings.

They may have lost a game or two
But the points took them to the top
They fought all the opposition
And saw many get the chop
Now they stand before us
On the Wembley turf at last
The crowd is right behind them
For goals that will come thick and fast
Cheltenham Town won't be forgotten
Once ninety minutes has been played
A silver cup with bows and ribbons
Is theirs to be displayed.

Ray Hammond

WOMEN'S VIEW OF FOOTBALL

What's on the telly I want to know,
No more football or go go goal,
I want a telly football free,
No more Beckham or Giggsy,
No more saves or corner kicks,
No more scoring or back flips,
No more refs with whistles blowing,
Or football matches men are always going,
I protest it's so boring,
What's so great about footballers scoring?
All this fuss over a cup,
Why don't footballers just give up?
Football can't last forever,
Then at last men and women can talk together,
No more football butting in,
No more pubs and drinking,
After all what could men discuss,
If away died all this fuss,
Men and women would have to speak,
Then marriage councillors they'd have to seek,
I think football should end right now,
No ifs, buts, or how,
I think tomorrow would be a better place,
No more football one equal race,
No more quarrels whose team is best,
One life of peace and perfect rest,
No more chanting from the stands,
Who gives a heck where the football lands,
No more cares of red and yellow,
No more threats to bare or bellow,
No more men away at games,
No more learning footballers' names,
I think football's great don't you?
If there was no football what the hell would men do?

Kim Darwell

GARY LINEKER (1983-1992)

Gary Lineker
Started his career with Little Leicester
Gary Lineker, Gary Lineker, Gary Lineker.
Lethal finisher, goal scorer, goal maker,
Cross bar shaker and post smasher
Gary Lineker
Penalty box predator, beast in the box
Like a cunning sly old fox
Always running his socks
Gary Lineker, Gary Lineker
Don't mention salt and vinegar
'86 World Cup golden boot winner
Gary Lineker radio commentator
Gary Lineker and Vinnie Jones
Micky taker and funny bones
Gary Lineker
Win, lose or draw
He always knew the score
Gary Lineker and Wembley stadium
England and the English thank and cheer him
Magic memories he brings
Especially when England wins
Gary Lineker the football player
Been and seen in the Match of the Day
Been and seen on the Match of the Day
We take note to what he has to say
Gary Lineker BBC TV commentator
Gary Lineker the player, the playmaker, the predator
An FA Cup finalist loser
A good man no poser.

Ali Khan

ONE BALL

There's only one football, amazing but true,
Kicked back and forth from me to you,
To the lads from the school and your mates in the park
On long summer evenings until it gets dark.
But the ball doesn't rest when the players sleep,
It crosses the sea in a silent leap,
Fleeing the sunset it follows the day
And lands on the ground where the children play.
It travels the world with a kick and a roll
To the boy in the village who's standing in goal.
With the heat on his back and dust on his feet,
To the kids in the city who play in the street.
Where the ball represents all their hopes and ambition
To carry away on its endless mission.
Sometimes it's new and sometimes it's old
Sometimes it's given and sometimes sold,
It moves between stadium, garden and beach,
On a tide of excitement, the cup within reach,
Working its way through the clubs and the teams
To the day of days on the field of dreams.
And when it's all over, the world's number one
Kicks the ball to his eight year old son
Who passes it on to his school mates and friends,
So the ball goes on and the game never ends.

J A Grey

RIMETNISCING

50 now, but many years ago,
I was there
'66 Wembley Stadium,
Not a care
Banks, Hunt, Moore and Peters,
Charltons, two
Cohen, Wilson, back to back,
Where were you?

Father up in Blackpool,
With my mam
Guesthouse TV broken,
In a jam
Walk along the prom on,
Golden Mile
Rediffusion window screening,
Nobby's smile.

Irish, Scottish, Welsh or English,
One for all
Every other nationality,
Kicked by Ball
Hurstie's hand aloft in triumph,
German gloom
Wolstenholme's famous words forever,
British heirloom.

'Some people are on the pitch.
They think it's all over.
It is now!'

Derek Chamberlain

ONCE

Once the drinking did not matter
as his body was young and lean
and on passionate Saturday afternoons
he tortured the opposing team,
drifting contemptuously past players,
as illusive as a ghost.
Once, but now small crowds jeer
for with beer and time he's slowed.
Once he had a future
now he's left with only a past,
he thought he was immortal
but even mountains turn to dust.
Yes, the tide is coming in,
the sandcastle crumbling down,
now he drinks alone as
there are new heroes in town.
Once the hangovers were bearable,
the mirror always shows the truth,
bulging stomach, double chin,
beaten, lost in the mist of his youth.

Guy Fletcher

LIVERPOOL ARE SO COOL

In past days, they used to rule
With Keegan and Toshak
They were top of the pack
Clemence in goal
Saving the ball
Now there's young Fowler and Owen
Who can't stop scoring
There's big David James
Who's played so many games
Man Utd to stop
Liverpool to go top
They're beginning to crack
To finish second in the pack
To leave Liverpool clear
The title, so near
To win it, so great
I just pray, it's not too late.

Paul Goddard

LIVERPOOL 0 WIMBLEDON 1
1988 FA CUP FINAL

That didn't look convincing
But we'll take it all the same
Just put this away
And we're back in the game
And there is the great Aldo
To step up and win the day
The ball's put on the spot
He'll put it away
All around me quiet
Some people on their knees
Hold your breath if you want
Soon you'll be able to breathe
I don't believe what's happened
It's never happened before
Aldo's missed the penalty
Now we'll never score.

Tony Holland

THE HILLSBOROUGH DISASTER
LIVERPOOL V NOTTS FOREST

God sent you to heaven
'Cause you were so weak
And you couldn't speak
All this because you got crushed
Thanks to the crowds that were in a rush
All because you wanted to see them play
You are now not here today
Your faces will remain in our hearts
And those memories will never part
The crowd always gives a cheer
But people still live in fear
Nobody knows who's to blame
Which leaves their families in pain
But we all think the police *are* to blame.

Toni Caddock (13)

FA CUP DAY

It's FA Cup day, the nation cheers,
Shouting at the telly and drinking beers.
A historical day about football and pride,
Feeling the build up excite you inside.
The ups, the downs, the in-betweens,
The greatest prize will fuel both teams.
Up a ramp between twin towers,
Walking through confetti showers.
Praying that we just might see
A couple of goals and victory.
Into the box the ball is played,
A man steps up and a goal is made.
Thousands of fans, they shout and they scream
Then calm down to encourage the team.
The referee's whistle, it rings out loud,
Causing a cheer from some in the crowd.
United were brave, better days they've had,
As fathers turn to sons and say 'Never mind lad.'
But they went all the way beating the best
So there is no shame in losing this test.
That just leaves the winners to pick up their prize
Lifting the cup brings tears to some eyes.
A magnificent trophy, the most famous in sport
A symbol of success in a battle well fought.

Ashley Gilbert
(An Arsenal Supporter)

ADRENALINE RUSH

Adrenaline rush as you enter the gate
Watching the team lose, win, what fate
No matter what we go back for more
For the ball in the net yea- *score*

The excitement running down the field
When the player scores he won't yield
A game of enjoyment dear to the heart
For young and old they'll never to part.

Anne Silcock

WEMBLEY REMEMBERED

After ninety minutes we feared the worst
Then came the hat trick by Geoff Hurst
Extra time the fans in clover
Spilled on the pitch they thought it over.

Banks, Wilson, Cohen and little Nobby
World Cup winners with captain Bobby
Hurst, Peters, Charlton, Ball
Household names and heroes all.

With big Jack and Roger Hunt
The mighty Germans they did blunt
The cup held high for the world to see
The year '66, the place Wembley.

Nineteen twenty-three the records endorse
The first Wembley final, that famous white horse
Bolton were winners the cup came alive
Now finals at Wembley number seventy and five.

To see the stars at Wembley is such a great sight
Ghosts from the past like Finney, Matthews, Wright
Names you remember stand out from the rest
Man Utd's forward line Law, Charlton, and Best.

There's been Toshack and Keegan and Steve Heighway too
Hunter, Giles and Bremner to name just a few.
There's been many a battle at the theatre of dreams
Names like Busby, Revie and Shankly have managed the teams.

Thousands of fans and millions on tele
Have thrilled at the skills of Eusabio and Pele
To tell the whole story would go on for hours
Of all the great happenings between the twin towers.

If you've been to a final and been heard to say
That was a moment of history, when I walked Wembley way.

S Williams

THE LOCAL DERBY

The passion, the pride,
Defeat, how I cried,
It's Derby Day and we just haven't tried,

But the victory elation,
A standing ovation,
Now that's Derby Day exhilaration.

John Norman-Daley

WE DID IT

I could cry,
I could weep,
I could run down the street,
I could dance,
I could sing,
I could be anything.

The boys have done it
They really have,
We're going to the twin towers,
To shout and scream
And sit on the edge of our seats
For one and a half hours,

On I can't wait
Until the phone line's free
So I can book my ticket to Wembley.

Lisa Reynolds (16)

CUP OF DREAMS

The FA Cup is up for grabs
Nothing unexciting nothing drab
Football players sweat it out
Knocking the football all about
Celebrating happy years
All the crowd give plenty cheer.

The FA Cup we celebrate
75 years to this very date
For every player what a dream
Just to be on the winning team.

P Henriksen

AN ODE TO THE ROBINS

Well it all started in '97
With Mr Cotterill's fantastic 11
Now everyone at the Robins is wearing a smile
And thinking of Wembley all the while
I went at 8.30am to queue at the door
At 10.00am they gave out a roar
I bought a ticket for my Wembley seat
And put it away so careful and neat
Now for a ticket to get on the bus
I knew by now there were thousands of us
So now I am ready for the 17th May
When the Robins are heading Wembley way
So Mr Cotterill, my man
Take your fantastic 11 and do what you can
If we win we'll all be so glad
But if we don't, we won't be too sad
We'll take off our hats to you and say
Remember that glorious day in May.

Caroline O'Connell

OUR LOCAL TEAMS

My friend and I were followers of our local football teams.
The Lilywhites at Preston and Blackburn Rovers were the dream.
We used to join in loudly with crowds and we would sing
About the great Tom Finney and Bryan Douglas on the wings
It didn't cost that much to go as it does nowadays
If it did we'd be going once a year
With money we got paid.

Mabel Harrison

MATCH OF THE DAY

I feel quite honoured and rather proud
that some of my words may be read by the crowd
So I had a think, about what I could write
and thought of the fans on a Saturday night
Whether at home, or out at a club
or merely supping a pint in the pub
Discussing the match, as only fans do
each of them telling the ref what to do
You'll notice now, I'm being polite
I have to remember who will read what I write
Did you see the linesman waving madly?
He said our Graeme had tackled badly
I must admit, he went in hard
but the ref should never have shown him the card
What about that shot that just went wide?
And Alan Shearer was never offside
How about that save from Flowers today?
I don't know how he pushed it away
And did you see that foul on Slater
He took his number and got him later!
The ref was a pain, he whistled and blew
for every little incident, he didn't have a clue
Mind you he was right about the free kick
And although Chris Sutton took it quick
It didn't go in and that was a shame
The whistle's blown now, it's the end of the game
I'll just finish me beer and then I'm away
Going to watch it again on Match of the Day.

M Russell

THE MATCH

Saturday night, the match is on,
My dad has turned the telly on,
Drinking whisky, eating nuts,
Eager to know who'll win,
Our team's losing, what a din!
Supporters disappointed, so's our dad
Mum and I look up and say
'Don't worry they'll win another day!'

Wednesday night, the match is banned
Angry supporters grow out of hand,
The ref takes the team back off, they're in despair
As supporters' missiles hurtle through the air
The faithful supporters all shout and jeer,
'When will our team be back out here?'

Zoë Downs (10)

THE BUZZ

The moment the ball
entered the net was
like no other.
There was nothing
to compare.
This wasn't a new
experience, he'd just
learned to savour it more,
as the years passed by.
All those outside
the game simply,
didn't understand.
How could they?
Only pros like him
knew that each strike
censored that spectre
of impending retirement.
Every goal postponed
thoughts of that
dreaded day when this
buzz would be given
the red card forever.

Paul Kelly

LEADING SCORER

It's what each football club desires,
A footballer that never tires,
A Giggs, a Beckham or a Scholes,
Or one that's always scoring goals.

The teams we follow they don't know,
Of the talent in the second row
Each chance of goal the striker's missed,
Adds another to his list,
He sits there like a garden gnome but he'd,
Have volleyed that one home,

With every game his total mounts,
There's another chance he counts
He even scores, while in the pub
But never picked, not even sub,
He is leading scorer in the land,
He must be worth a million grand,
This scorer will be never seen
To tread the turf that's oh so green
But next time that you hear him shout
You'll pick him out, there is no doubt.

Ian Evans

FOOTBALL FAN GRANNY!

'Football's on TV tonight.'
'Oh not *again*' I sighed.
'I'll miss Coronation Street - again,
And Brookside too' - I could have cried.
But the match came on, regardless,
And glumly I got out my sewing . . .
The whistle blew - the game began,
'Where's that player going?'
The family got very vocal,
As chances of goals were lost.
'He's useless' 'Where did they get *him?*'
'Obviously at not much cost!'
Now, I knew nothing of football -
And gradually got very bored.
But, suddenly - things got exciting -
It seemed that someone had scored!
So, I started to try and get involved -
'Who's he? Which one is which?'
'Who's playing in the blue shirts?'
'Why has he gone off the pitch?'
Not a good move - I'm told I'm interrupting'
'Be quiet and watch the match.'
So I really tried to understand
That only the *goalie* can catch!
. . . But now, as years have drifted by,
I've really become quite a fan!
And proved the point, without a doubt,
That football is *not* just for *man!*

June Bootle

SIXTY-EIGHT

Who could forget that golden day,
Scarves trailing down the motorway,
And then the slow suburban crawl
To reach the greatest goal of all?

The stadium that plays the part
Of soccer's living, beating heart,
Where ghostly greats are all around
Still buoyed up on a sea of sound.

The flags, the chants, the greenery,
The tidal wave of ecstasy,
Who could resist that atmosphere
And fail to smile and fail to cheer?

And when the players strode in view
Such thunder rolled and pennants flew,
And people danced and waved and sang,
Until the air around us rang.

A spell was cast inspiring all
To cheer or groan at every ball,
As patterns flowed across that sea
Of legend-haunted greenery.

Until the moment came - a goal!
Whoever heard such thunder roll?
Vesuvius had blown its top,
I thought the roar would never stop.

And when the cup was lifted high
A tear was misting every eye,
Regret for fans of Everton
And joy, West Bromwich Albion.

. . . Such memories of sixty-eight,
I know why they call Wembley great.

David C Harris

KING OF THE KOP

Kenny Dalglish (former footballing ace!)
Suddenly found he couldn't stick the pace
Appointed back in '85 to keep the Liverpool legend alive
He was haunted by Hysel, horrifying Hillsborough then came
Liverpool were big, but not bigger than the game!
Dalglish seldom looked happy, he was moody and mean
His only comfort the dug out on which he'd lean
Had that golden smile when he used to score
Deserted his face for evermore?
Some say his interest of late had ceased
And of course Tony Adams had been released
John Barnes said he needed a change of scene
More like 'loads of lire' know what I mean
Beardsley in and out of the side
The meddling media hurt Kenny's pride
A boardroom bust-up with speedie signing
Yet still no hint of Dalglish resigning!
Then out of 'the blue' he caused a sensation
The Everton draw, then the resignation
Did he do it for the club or for himself?
Perhaps he did it because of ill health
An impeccable record, retired at the top
Kenny's abdicated as king of the Kop!

Pash

FA CUP FINAL DAY

Here we go again
It's the middle of May,
Arsenal meet Newcastle
On FA Cup Final Day

There'll be nerves and there'll be jitters
And legs will get all trembley,
As the two teams march out
On the great pitch at Wembley

It's the seventy fifth time
That the final is played here,
Let's hope that the teams
Give us all something to cheer

The noise will be deafening
When the fans begin to roar,
As they wait for their team
To open up the score

They'll play with skill and determination
And dig deep into their souls,
With Bergkamp and Shearer
There's bound to be some goals

But there can only be one winner
Let's hope it's football on the day,
So we can come back next year
When two more teams will play

So that's it - end of season
But don't look down now - chin up
Or have you forgotten
We still have the world cup!

Matthew Robins

THE FOOTBALL FABLE

Steeped in history and folklore too,
With villains and heroes always on view,
Depending on supporters' points of view,
So it's up for the Cup for Dad and his lad,
Both trusting their spirits won't be low,
All teams in the Cup need a little luck,
Some of it good, some of it bad,
For Aston Villa it was all so sad,
After winning the Cup 'twas lost to a jack-the-lad,
When he nicked it from a local shop,
Even the coppers accepted the loss,
Now we have the modern game,
With all its heroes the kids can name,
From the little minnows, to the majestic and mighty,
The games are played, daytime or nightly,
The hopes and fears, players' joy and tears,
Magic moments and memories, that last for years,
New modern hype and glamour reign supreme,
It's every schoolboy's Wembley dream,
Those twin entrance towers like a magnet stand
Attracting supporters from far away lands
For the Royals and commoners, one and all,
A day at Wembley - it's a ball.

T Nicholls

THE MAGIC OF THE CUP

Every year I feel the same I don't
know why it's just a game, the
heartfelt pain when we go out the
moans and cries and wails and
shouts, this anguish that I feel inside
it's something that I can't describe.
So why do I carry on, hoping,
praying, willing them on. I'll tell
you why I do this my friend, because
when you win it's a different ball-game.
The passion that you feel inside, your
lungs ready to burst with pride, the
magical walk up Wembley Way as
the sun comes out it will be our
day, one nil down two one up the
final whistle we've won the Cup, so
why does it mean so much, who
knows that's the magic of the Cup.

Emanuel Brady

Late Season Blues

O we really mustn't talk of relegation,
Although each week our team contrives to lose;
It's six weeks or even seven since they got a shot on goal,
And we'd gladly swap our strike force for a Shearer or a Cole.
But - let's be nice to them,
And not ascribe *all* vice to them,
They're doing their best to bring us better news;
Although our goalie's rather short,
And quite the worst we've ever bought,
We must get behind our favourite Blues.

O we mustn't even mention relegation,
And let us not the management abuse;
Our senior coach has sworn that he will fight to his last breath,
But will the Chairman's vote of confidence become the kiss of death?
Well - let's all blame the ref,
He's not just blind, he's Mutt and Jeff,
And obviously biased in his views;
His personal habits are obscene,
And on him we will vent our spleen -
But let's get behind our favourite Blues.

O we mustn't even *think* of relegation,
To play those lesser teams we'd just refuse;
Though we're getting ever closer to the dreaded 'last three' line,
We'll keep defending stoutly with our trusty flat back nine.
So - let's avoid the drop,
The rot has simply got to stop!
A goal or two would light our heroes' fuse;
Though Europe's a forgotten dream,
We love our hopeless, useless team -
So let's get behind our favourite Blues!

Geoffrey V Willis

POSITIONING

Midfield General, entrenched, standing central,
Eye-line just above the crossbar,
Eye-line just behind the goal-line,
Somewhere still on a last muddy terrace
Of poppy-red shirts, of blood red
Voices spilling onto, spilling
Out and into a winter's un-flood-lit

No man's land. And his great grandson, I,

Just a few feet wide, not sat at his right
Hand, but stood on his left, planted
And growing on a knee-high, step-
Wide, worn, wooden box, planted and calling
For long balls (in) and through balls (through),
On his left and directing shouts
At Directors, rifling shots at the Board.

Midfield General, Christmas 1914,
Striking and lighting one small match,
His rattling voice and Gatling breath
Hacking smoke white ghosts into evening air,
Ghosts crossing the pitch black silence
Of night, uniting with *Stille*
Nacht echoes of cities' bombed streets, and I,

Just there, a few feet wide, and clad not in
This season's kit, but buttoned, like
He, in collarless shirt, neither
Red nor blue; eye-line just back from the goal-
Line, eye-line not quite past the side-
Line, and together we, Midfield
General and I, Great Grandfather and I,

Take up positions on no man's land.

Robert Bradshaw

JUST A GAME

We were in the final minute, both teams had failed to score,
The ball went for a corner, the crowd set up a roar,
The kick was hard, the ball went high, the players pushed and shoved,
The heads went up, a fist was used, the Keeper? No he's gloved,
A penalty was awarded, the cheers and groans combined,
The ref. he was surrounded, but he wouldn't change his mind,
The ball was placed upon the spot, a deathly hush descended,
The penalty taker v the Keeper, on them the Cup depended,
The Kicker ran up to the ball, and placed it to the right,
The Goalie dived the other way, the game was out of sight,
Half the ground erupted, in ecstatic noisy cheers,
The other half was silent, their eyes were filled with tears,
The ref. he blew his whistle, the cup was won and lost,
Directors in their padded seats, were counting up the cost,
And when the dust had settled, and both sides go from
                                        whence they came,
There's bound to be a wag who says, 'Aye, Fitba's just a game.'

R Penman

FOOTBALL IS THE GAME

Call yourself a fan?
Call yourself a freak
Football is the game,
That makes everyone unique.

Know everything, about every club,
Or is it just one team?
Football is the game,
That is always full of dreams.

Whether you're old and grey,
Or young, lonely and fat,
Football is the game,
That is all *'that'*

We are all led to believe,
That refs. are always right.
Football is the game,
That starts many fights.

Rinaldo, Ince, Beckham, Butt
Players from the best.
Football is the game,
Leagues above the rest.

Rachel Edwards

WEMBLEY

The stadium of golden memories
Going back to twenty three
The stage of many a drama
Acted out for you and me

The elation of success
Mingled with the agony of defeat
The result of the battle
When the two survivors meet

Instant heroes are made
With the kick of a ball
They enter the Wembley hall of fame
Where many a legend stands tall

To hold the cup aloft
And hear the roar of the crowd
To hold a cup winners medal
Truly a moment to be proud

Yet the greatest moment came
Over thirty years ago
When England beat the world
And many a tear did flow

Dear old Wembley Stadium
The home of the English game
You have a place within many a heart
And should receive deserved acclaim

Paul Philip Brooks

THE FOOTBALL 'WIDOW'

She was a martyr to football, lonely and sad,
For most of her life football claimed dad.

No matter what the weather, rain, hail or shine,
She knew in her heart, he'd spin her a line,

'Lads are all going,' he'd say looking sad,
She'd sigh, 'I'll get your flask ready,
But I'm still pretty mad.'

This situation went on year after year,
Mum weathered the relegation battles, dad used to fear.

She didn't mind the days when matches were won,
He was as happy as Larry and twice the fun.

One day he came in, grinning from ear to ear,
They were top of the League now,
And he was full of good cheer.

But it was hard at the top,
The club's results were up then down,
Dad's hair fell out and he wore a permanent frown.

Then it came to my wedding, oh, dear me,
Dad's face was a picture, I should have left that day free.

Why hadn't I checked the fixtures for that day,
The lads were at home so he couldn't give me away.

His team won the League, and he was one big smile,
But it was too late in the day for him to take me down the aisle.

Joan Creary

UP THE SPURS

All through the years I've loved it,
No woman could stand in the way
All my joys and pleasures
Are watching Tottenham play.
I've followed them for years now
Hark hear the cockerel crow
Up the Spurs, come on you lads
That shout we love and know.
Years of classy players
Plenty of FA Finals too.
Our support we'll always give,
We have true faith in you.
Jimmy Greaves the hero star
His memory will live on
Campbell and Hoddle, Walker and Waddle
And all the players that shone,
This is really British
And British is the best,
Forget about the other sports
Don't bother with the rest.
The game is very special
But half-time snacks are not
In sun and rain in health and pain
To the match I'm gone like a shot.
I'm football crazy, I'm football mad.
I'll remember with fondness
Of the joys of the game I've had.
Although I'm eighty-three now
The game still charges my heart,
To sit and be a spectator
Yes that is the very best part
I've been a fan for many years
And seen the rejoicing and many tears!

Silver Fox

THE MATCH

Football is a truly wonderful sport,
Just ask anyone what team they support.
Fans in club colours, and all chanting together,
There night or day, whatever the weather.
So proud, it's an honour to be at a match.
You have to shout loud, if they hit a bad patch.
All together the team play their part,
In making this game a form of technical art,
Total commitment from players and fans.
Make this the best game in the land,
The referee is a man, I dare to mention,
I'm afraid his decisions are often up for question,
The manager is a remarkable man,
Chewing and shouting out the game plan.
One goal down, the pressure is on,
Time for a change, the game has to be won.
New pair of legs, he's past the back four,
It's a *goal*, the fans want more.
Chances missed, lots of ooh's and ahh's.
The fans all chant for their favourite stars.
Hoping the winning goal will come
It's too late, the whistles' gone.

Anne Sackey

WEMBLEY STADIUM

Wembley Stadium, in all it's glory
Tells us all a special story
The Old Twin Towers, a hall of fame
Of the greatest players in the game
Charlton, Rush, George Best too,
Football's elite, to name but a few
FA Cup Final Day, Wembley the host
This place is the best, that it can boast
Every club has a chance, no matter their size
The FA Cup is the ultimate prize
Wembley Stadium, arena of dreams
The apex of soccer, or so it seems
It's Cup Final Day, the supporters are here
All merry with song, oh what an atmosphere
The place is alive, the fans are roaring
Great players they come, dreaming of scoring
Football, football, a way of life for some
Supporting their team, hoping to come
To the famous Wembley Stadium.

Wayne Mantle

TWIN TOWERS MAGIC

In the first ever Cup Final at Wembley
The game kicked off forty-five minutes late.
In those days it wasn't an all-ticket affair
And far too many turned up at each gate.

Bolton was the name that went on the trophy
When they defeated West Ham by two nil.
But this final is always best remembered
For the antics of a white horse called Bill.

Nineteen-twenty-seven was a special year,
The only time 'our' cup left England.
'Cos the winners that day were Cardiff City,
There's no doubt Plaid Cymru thought it was grand.

Nineteen-thirty the Graf Zeppelin flew over,
Nineteen-forty-six was the year the ball burst.
Bert Turner was the first to score for both sides
Nineteen-fifty-three was Stan Matthews' first.

Seventy-five glorious years at Wembley
Deserve to be celebrated in rhyme.
It's everyone's ambition to play there.
Perhaps it may be your team's turn next time.

R Gordon

RED AND WHITE FLAME

A rocket is launched
From Seaman to the feet of Wright.
Highbury is entranced,
On the threshold of a miracle.

Time and motion burn
With a red and white flame today,
The ball is burning
But watch! Wright steals the oxygen.

One touch,
Here we go.
The blaze arcs over Jackson.
Evertonian!
Only to dance magically on.

With clock suspended,
Beauty free from gripping arrest,
The ball's in the net!
Southall and thousands are bemused.

Now here comes the roar,
The four-sided lion's in full voice,
'Ian Wright, Wright, Wright!'
Time
You can breathe life into time.

Stephen Wren

HEART IS WHERE THE HOME IS

Oh Arsenal, Arsenal, what a place,
Full of style and class and grace.
Ian 'three names' the crowd adore,
They are, all hoping he will score.
So I sit, feeling bored and guilty as well,
As the Highbury crowd begins to swell.
The game 'kicks off' the gunners score!
And I look around; 'O what a bore'
Do not, get me wrong, football I love,
As I stare at the celestial night sky above,
You see this poem really is a scam,
My sons support Arsenal and I support West Ham!
The crowd hold their breath; 'Wrighty is hurt.'
My son whispers, 'Dad can I have his shirt?'
I leap to my feet, with an ecstatic cry,
A few confused faces say, 'You're going to die,'
But sadly, I cannot tell them all
That the Hammers have just pulled back to two-all.
I decide that in future, 'Just a little cheer,'
With the radio, firmly 'glued' to my ear.
So very soon my duty is done,
And the children go with their friends to have fun.
So I can now stop, my north London roam
And return to the place, that I can call home
Where I can sing my 'Bubbles' song
And be, where I feel, I belong
Oh Arsenal, Arsenal, full of grace.
It is not my style, it is not my place.

Terry Sains

WEMBLEY CUP FINALS

They were there in nineteen-twenty three
The one where history was made.

Although they lost the final that day
Just remember how they played.

Back again in 'sixty-four'
They came up trumps this time

They beat brave Preston by 3 to 2
The winner in injury time

In seventy-five they won again
By beating Fulham two-nil

With both goals coming from young Taylor
Like a predator waiting to kill

The last time they won it came as a shock
To Gunners fans young and old

For masterful Trevor headed the winner
So Bonzo had the cup to hold . . .

Which team?

West Ham United . . .

David Lowe

GOING FOR THE DOUBLE

I've spent the spring screaming
while others were dreaming
of fates far less lofty than this -
screaming at the TV
and at Highbury,
screaming at each narrow miss.

Going for the Double
is nothing but trouble,
the stress more than my heart can stand,
from penalty showdowns
and grim one-nil hoe-downs
at stadia all over the land.

I can't bear to be there,
I can't bear to be here,
at home where I've been put on cable.
If my eight-year-old son
weren't himself a Young Gun
I'd be drinking us under the table.

While my five-year-old daughter
who gets tipsy on water
dances round in an Arsenal scarf,
my son and myself
find the strain on our health
leaves us almost unable to laugh.

But our team are the best -
what's it like for the rest,
for whom each new defeat is a blow?
For the dream of the Double
takes me out of my troubles -
I'm high just as much as I'm low.

Deborah Collins

WOR LADS FOR THE CUP

Howay the Lads
We can see you gannin'
Doon the Road to Wembley,
Where we will all be standing.
To watch you with pride and joy
As you walk on the field
To kick the arse of Arsenal
And watch the Gunners yield.

Whether on the terrace or in the Bar
Or in our own armchair
Our hearts will all be with you
As you take the field doon there
With Batty, Pearce and Shearer,
And all the Magpies' lads
We've got the team to win the Cup
Best chance we've ever had.

Howay the lads
We can see you gannin'
Doon the road to Wembley
Where we will all be standing
And we'll be cheering all the day
'Cos goals we'll have a-many
When you kick the arse from *Arse--nil*
They'll have *nil* and that's not *any*.

Howay the lads
We can see you gannin'
Doon the road to Wembley
Where we will all be standing.
And we'll support you all the way
And when you come back home
The Cup held high in victory
Well, you'll know you weren't alone.

V Lackenby

WORLD CUP

Here we go again, heading for France,
Hoping to lead the best a merry dance
Dare we return home having lost the day,
Not according to Shearer, he'll make them pay.

What about Owen do you think he'll score
Not many he will miss.
I know someone who could score four
I think he's known as Tiss.

Poor old Chris finds it hard to think
Was it worth it to call in Madam
He seemed to have faith in calling a shrink
I think he should call in Adams.

What a great sport this is, the sport of Kings,
The colours, the sighs, crescendo of the crowd,
'Penalty', 'Pass', 'Foul', 'Give it to the wing'!
Cheers, Boos, goals in praise so loud.

I've only just realised, and, it's true to say
Without a round thing most games couldn't play
Not tennis, not cricket, not golf at all
All of them round, just like the football.

Win or lose we praise their name
So proud we were to be part of the game
Now if ever I am Born Again
Let it be near to Bramhall Lane.

This game is not only, to play for winnings,
We are proud to participate, we had an innings.

James McCarthy

A SMALL DISCREPANCY

Aw wor enjoying mi pint at th' local, abaat a few weeks ago,
When a lad wi a jersey ov Leeds United spock-up,
He sed, 'Thas net a supporter anole?'
Well a told him, 'Leeds!, Thas a barn pot, thas net a team, thas a joke.'
'Th' best team's Uddersfield Town, just tak a look at th' pictures
                                                            on th' wall.'
Th' young whipper snapper laughed an chunted, tawkin
                                                a European glory days,
Aw says, 'Uddersfield could be playing in Europe.'
He says, 'Aye, if th' wor a world war today.'
Aw sed, 'Anyway, Europe means nowt, especially to th'
                                        greatest teams thas ever
Played. Yo see th' FA Cup's th' trophy tha Europeans wish
                                                they could play.'

A know Uddersfield aw've net won it, for as long as yo
                                            heeard th' name.
But bringing it home in 21-22, it wor history they wor
                                            making tha day.'
For Uddersfield lifted tha tropy, wi pride of West Yorksher, 'Hurray!'
An shadows wor cast over Alifax, Bradford, Leeds, oh an Bradford PA

An yes, a con see wor ya say lad,
It's bin longer than seventy five years,
An yor probably reight, it wan't a Wembley site,
Whear the game wor won tha day.
But to us is human tha small discrepancy,
However yo view th' cost.
But at least yo con say tha on our day, we won tha FA Cup!

Richard M Durrans

THE DAY RON RADFORD SCORED

Hereford played Newcastle
In an FA Cup replay
MacDonald said he'd score ten
Hereford would pay
It took eighty minutes
A cross, MacDonald soared
He thought it was the winner
Until Ron Radford scored.

Radford won a tackle
And then played a one-two
Then there wasn't any doubt
What he was going to do
A bulging net, ecstatic crowd
On the pitch they poured
They were celebrating
The goal Ron Radford scored.

So Hereford beat Newcastle
In that FA Cup 3rd Round
It will never be forgotten
By all those in the ground
Each year on 3rd Round day
That goal is not ignored
Everyone remembers
The day Ron Radford scored.

Robert Brailsford

TO THE HOLY GRAIL

It's the famous FA cup story,
75 years of footballing glory.
Anything can happen, anything goes,
Desire and passion, highs and lows.
True David and Goliath battles,
Always fill the news,
Everyone has different views.

'That was a penalty!'
'It wasn't in the box!'
'That wasn't a foul!'
'He should have been sent off!'

For 90 minutes, different people come together,
To support their team and betray them never.
Strangers unite, families divide,
All for the love of a football side.
The result can make you strong,
It can make you weak
Make your day,
Or destroy your week.
Ready to boast or ready to hide,
Wanting to live, wanting to die.

Emotions felt and experienced,
On this bumpy road.
Only two make it,
And there's no second goes.
On the road to the holy grail,
For 90 minutes of anticipated glee.
And sing 'Kay sera, sera,
We're going to Wembley!'

Geraldine Musajjakawa

SHATTERED DREAMS

What joy is there in excavating the soul?
In digging up fading dreams and lost passions,
In the hope of somehow restoring their past glory.

Past legacies burning bright,
Serve as my guiding flame,
As I dare to hope a hopeless dream,
The dream lives on, as yet unfulfilled.

What have I done to spite cruel fate?
For see what fate has decreed.
To wander through the ruins of a once proud tradition,
Now sucked into a whirlpool of greed and decay.
Once glittering trophies, remnants of a forgotten era,
Lie broken in the dust.

Can it be a game and just a game
Which moves us to such magnitude?
We cheer, we cry, we jeer and we laugh.
A maelstrom of emotion,
Which can twist and turn at the kick of a ball.

But most of all is the feeling of love,
When we remember the days that started it all.
A young boy playing with his father in the garden.
Standing for the first time on the terraces and gazing down,
At our idols and heroes.
And we dreamed,
And we dreamed.

Jonathan Citrin

THE REFEREE

Now listen here you young man,
I'm in charge, so I'll give you a ban.
I'll not stand, for any foul play,
It's an early bath, do you hear what I say.
Right on with the game, it's their free kick,
Stand well back, did you hear, is this some
kind of trick.
This here whistle is a waste of time,
I blow it and blow it, but you don't give a
dime,

Lovely tackle lad, that's the way,
Now take it forward, keep them at bay.
Oh dear me, you're not listening at all,
We play this game by kicking the ball.
I think you'd like to join your friend,
He's having an early bath go on the end.

Kenneth Town

BOLTON WANDERERS

They play attractive football,
Their footwork is a dream
Their name is Bolton Wanderers
And they are my favourite team.

When they first won the FA Cup
I was still only a lad
But since then I've followed Wanderers
Through good times and through bad.

I used to go to Burnden Park
That's where they played their game
But now they have a new place
Raebok Stadium is the name.

Wolves, West Brom and Ipswich
Were taken in their stride
And if we scored the winning goal
It filled my heart with pride.

On Saturday's I'd check results
And really was delighted
If I saw my favourite team
Had licked Manchester United.

I can't get down to watch them now
But still I cheer them on
And when I see them win a game
Shout, 'Well done lads, well done.'

Wilfred Flitcroft

SIR STANLEY MATTHEWS

Mesmerising on the wing, our Stan,
Was football's finest gentleman,
In his England shirt he looked so neat,
Shorts long and baggy, his magic feet,
A shimmy to the left, a ghost to the right,
Fullbacks he beat from morning to night.

His finest hour in fifty-three,
The FA Cup Final at Wembley,
Blackpool beat Bolton and Stan had a blinder,
3-1 down and here's a reminder,
On the wing he just couldn't be caught,
As he set up goals 2 and 3 for Mort,
With the final whistle about to go,
Stan's final bow, legs in full flow,
Again the fullback beaten for fun,
Then Perry scored, the Cup was won,
For Stan a dream come true at last,
We can but reflect on football's past.

Geraint Graves

SATURDAY AT THREE

On Saturday at three,
Grown men become free,
For it's kick off time,
And the fans are sublime.

All over the nation,
There's anticipation,
Will the Reds dominate?
Can the Blues retaliate?

The game is now away,
The ball at last in play,
The roar of the great crowd,
Is incredibly loud.

The action gets faster,
One team is the master,
The ball finds the net,
Some rejoice, others fret.

The opponents despair,
They don't have enough flare,
Impossible to score!
They can offer no more.

The final whistle blows,
And everyone there knows,
That's it for the week,
They return to being meek.

The ground empties out,
It's quiet now, no shout,
Yet another great game,
Win or lose it's the same.

J O'Boyle

GIANT MINNOW

Every year little team's dream,
Sometimes these dreams come true,
Drawing a 'giant' in the Cup,
And finally, scraping through.

It does not happen often,
Usually once a year,
And little clubs rarely win,
Against a 'giant' from a higher tier.

Hereford against Newcastle in '72,
Dumping out Supermac,
Colchester v Leeds in '71,
Then there's no looking back.

Even when it's a barren year,
Remember, next time round,
There could be a shock in store,
So listen for the magical sound.

Terry Goodwin (13)

THE 75TH ANNIVERSARY

It's the FA Cup Final
In Wembley
The 75th
Anniversary.

The Magpies are kicking
They're on the ball.
They're in the final
Facing Arsenal.

So who's gonna win?
Let's wait and see
But Newcastle is
The team for me.

Claire Hall (12)

SATURDAY AFTERNOON

I stand there with complete concentration,
The passion inside exaggerates the importance to extreme proportions.
The excitement evoked by the display of sublime beauty.
The tension and atmosphere created by an almost insane collective
obsession.

Urgency increases as the minutes tick away,
More mental power is pushed into trying to make it happen
More vocal advice and encouragement is hurled out
The temperature is rising, the desire deepening.

Suddenly the break is on, they've found a way through,
Past one defender, then two, 'played lad', on to the left foot and,
'Time now, keep it down', the crowd erupts, it's finally there,
A wave of relief and ecstasy sweeps through the sea of red.

Anna Leah Ferdinando

ONCE UPON THE FA CUP TRAILS

Once upon the FA Cup trails
Came a team called Wrexham from the North of Wales.

The first round, we met Colwyn Bay
They may have been Giantkillers for the day.
But Yosser saved us 13 minutes from time
To throw us a much needed lifeline.
In the replay Yosser's goals helped the game to seal
And his winner came from a cheeky back-heel.

The second round was Scunthorpe, we thought our run had hit the wall
But we managed to come back and square it two-all.
In the replay, patience was the key
And we ended up winning two goals to three.

The third round brought West Ham to our home
The pitch covered in snow made Harry moan.
We took them to a replay at Upton Park
Where Kevin Russell left his mark.

A fourth round trip to Peterborough's home London Road
And between us six goals flowed.
They went 2-1 ahead again just after the break
But goals from Watkin and Rooster put the candles on our cake.

To the Midlands where Steve Bruce gave them the lead
                                    from a corner ball
And in the second half we made the mighty Brum fall.
Devlin was dismissed back to the dressing room
And goals from Yosser, Humes and Connolly ruined their afternoon.

Next came the big one at Saltergate
A second division team would have a semi-final date.
And so it was not to be
As Beaumont scored to Chesterfield's glee.

Here ends our FA Cup adventure for the year
We turned out to be the Giantkillers with no fear.

Paula Austin

IT'S ONLY A GAME

My mother said she didn't understand football.
She didn't understand the off-side rule.
She didn't understand why I wanted Sky Sports
She didn't understand what all the fuss was about.
It's only a game.

How, she asked, can people with Yorkshire and Cockney accents
                                        play for Ireland?
What is the sense in six different nationalities playing for a
                                        'London' club?
Why do people pledge loyalty to a team?
What's Tottenham to them or they to Tottenham
That they should weep for it?

Recently, she went to a World Cup match, Ireland against Belgium.
An agnostic amongst true believers, she joined in the hymns.
When Ray Houghton scored, she jumped on her seat
And the small change from her pocket scattered amongst
The plastic beer glasses.

There were no converts that night in the rain.
An Irish fan kissed a police horse. An elderly Belgian
Shrugged his shoulders and mispronounced 'Sorry'.
The Irish fans celebrated defeat with a chorus.
Heysel memories.

My mother still understands nothing of football
Except the perfect curve of the ball from Houghton's head
And the ripple of the net and maybe why once, at Christmas,
Terrace-hoarse voices echoed across No Man's Land.
Es ist nur ein Spiel.

Caitríona McDonagh

UNTITLED

Football is a funny old game
One day you play your best
The next time you're a complete mess
90 minutes of running about
Aiming for the back of the net
But all you do is become a complete get
All the hacking and illegal tackling
You just shouldn't do
As you seem to give the player
A free kick over you.

How many cards have you received
It's more than any boy I know has ever received
Club discipline is high
But your self discipline is low
You just don't know when to let go
Kicking and screaming all match through
People just wouldn't know it was you.

Time after time
Season after season
You find a very poor reason
Why it just wasn't your season.

Take a leaf out of your team mates' book
Then maybe you'll have a lot more luck
When you can keep those cards on a small tender hook
Making your team go by the book
Then playing our game in an all new look.

Suzan Ford

MOVING ON

All is quiet now
Only the sound of tired metal
Papers soaring in empty stands
The grass has time to settle

No more whistles, no more shouts
Oh such memories were had this day
Where have all the characters gone
The final act in a long running play

Long live the stadium
In my eyes it will never die
It is the house of my fondest memories
No matter how the developers will try.

Brian Deane

WARRIORS

The tribes are on the attack
This time they must surely win
Their honour they must reclaim
They call their compatriots home
Their chants are heard on the wind
The distant throng moves ever nearer
Their cry heightens the senses
In turn each warrior takes up the call
Over hills and all across the land
Steadily the hoard march on
Outsiders look on in awe
As united the throng move as one
One thought alone fills their mind
The battle about to be waged
As they round the final bend there
Before them their battle ground
Impelled by an unseen force
They move forward as one
To stand at last on hallowed ground
'Old Trafford' by name
Where battles are fought and won
Then when evening comes
They make their way home again
In triumph or despair
Reliving every second
Safe in the knowledge that
Next week they will
Triumph!

S L Pullen

LFC

I support the reds at home,
Playing their Mersey rival.
The adrenaline starts to pump,
The focus point flies through the air.
Attackers advance, defenders deny
The tool of the game goes up in the sky.

Past the centre the chants crescendo,
The black and white orb,
Goes out to the wing,
Slicing through the Mersey mist.
Dodging the blue defenders
A sliding tackle leaves an up-ender.

A free kick granted,
Several star shooters form a group,
The chance is taken, just too high.
Back on the field ready to fight,
Pass, dribble, pass
Glides across the grass.

The scoring group again
This time not in vain,
Soaring high, soaring in
Supporters create a natural din.

Sandra Shepherd

LIFE AND DEATH

November the ninth, I'll never forget,
The best and the worst day of my life yet,
Playing the Manks, biggest game of the season,
But, it didn't seem right for some terrible reason.

Straight to 'The Gunners' for beer and JD,
We head for the ground, 'Was that tannoy for me?'
The atmosphere's crackling with songs for the boys,
The sights, the smells, the usual noise,
The tannoy again, shrill and awake,
'It was for me, Butler,' there must be some mistake.

The marble halls, still got plenty of time,
A shiver of something runs down my spine,
Phone home is the message, what can it be?
I could never have guessed the news waiting for me,
Mum answers the phone with the worst news of all,
'Get home,' she's quiet while I play the fool.

Three fifty pm it says on the clock,
The beer and the whiskey numb most of the shock,
On the way to the tube, the ticket touts bait,
'Two hundred quid for your seat',
'Yeah, right, fuck off mate',
The news tries its best to get in to my brain,
The fact that I won't see my Dad again.

I know the league title is all dreams and stuff,
But this season's different, it just won't be enough,
November the ninth, Dad I'll never forget you.
The worst day of my life, we beat them 3 - 2.

Ian D Harkess

LIVERPOOL VERSES NEWCASTLE UNITED

Red is our home colour,
And yellow is away,
But no matter what we're wearing,
Our best is what we play.

With Fowler on the team,
And Owen and McAteer,
Newcastle had no chance,
They played the game in fear.

When the whistle went for kick off,
Berger started the game,
He ran straight past Batty,
Who just stood there in shame.

At the end of the match,
It was a draw,
But extra time was given,
Will anyone score?

Macca crossed it to Owen,
Who took a classic shot,
He wanted to score a goal,
And that's exactly what he got.

The final score was 2-0,
Liverpool's won the game,
Fowler scored the final goal,
Newcastle's lost again.

Candida Carcel (14)

THIRTIES EWOOD

Along Bolton Road to Ewood, crowds walked
Or from Boulevard took a tram car ride,
About forthcoming match everyone talked
All eager to watch Blackburn's well known side.

When a big game involved the boys in blue
Youngsters sat around pitch near touch-lines,
On Kidder Street roofs, folk climbed for a free view
Whilst spectators on terrace smoked Woodbines.

Game in the thirties differed from today
Goalies wore flat caps, were charged in the net,
Accepted as normal part of the play
Plus heavy leather ball, hard to kick when wet.

Roundabout the middle of that decade
Ewood's faithful hadn't much to cheer,
Rover's form started to decline and fade
Relegation became very real fear.

Lost to 'Stanley' in Cup, down to 'Div' two
Bob Crompton took over gave fans a shout,
New signings, his team in stature grew
Good Cup run, promoted, then war broke out.

Bringing thirties football to an end
Friendly rivalry started to disappear,
Playing and watching took another trend
Witty banter went with the atmosphere.

Raymond Winston Aspden

ONE NILL TO THE ARSENAL
(In early season 1997/98, Ian Wright surpassed Cliff Bustin's record of more than half a century as Arsenal's greatest ever marksman)

Chance after chance after chance went by
The elusive chase for the second coming
And for every such chance that went so grazingly wide
'Twas the decibel ditty of 'haha-hoos'
Their 'haha-hoos' and 'haha-hoos'
The faithful's chants to a near goal.

And with their rearguard arsenal blazing in fire
Denying the enemy the whiff of a chance
To rid the right that Wright had writ
As 'twas on the first ever victory to glory
(Sh sh - Sheffield United are still ruing their luck to this day!)
One nil to the Arsenal 'twas all but set be
Till the final whistle, the cherished prize.

They left their hallowed halls of Highbury on a high
For having buried one more team under the whirlpool
Who cares about goal difference
Or the enemy's epithet of 'boring, boring Arsenal'
With three points in the bag and table ascent
And scent of the summit in scenes of bliss.

Can this be the season of glory revisited
To realise the team's Biblical billing
According to holy writ in the book of Job (38:22-23)
As in particular of 'Have you seen the Arsenal!'
An acclamation of adoration?

And is the league season not a sprint but a marathon
We can only but take one day at a time
And one nil to the Arsenal is enough unto the day.

Benjamin Takavarasha

WHO NEEDS FOOTBALL? 1923 - 1998

Who needed football in 1923?
Wembley in its heyday was the place to be
Our grandfathers and ancestors
Founded this great hobby
Bolton Wanderers v West Ham was the FA to see.

Who needed football in 1939?
Tickets were 15 shillings for the final tie
4-1 to Portsmouth against Wolves
Was the bet to buy
Lucky Mr Harvey, a draper's shop, did run
Displayed the cup for two weeks
For he gave a suit to every Pompee
That scored a goal that day.

Who needed football in 1953?
Harry Hutchinson of Sunderland
For his house was painted red and white you see
His scarf he wouldn't part with,
And 'They buried him with thee.'

Who needs football in 1998?
After 75 years of playing, you and I need football
It's a healthy outdoor sport
And so does Gary Lineker, go on give us one report
Come on Arsen Venger, please smile and give it some
Come on Newcastle, we're having so much fun!
Whoever wins the final,
Let's give the final cheer and say
'Congratulations football is always here to stay!'

M Mullett

FOOTBALL PRAYER

The cold air stings my cheeks,
The cheering hurts my throat,
My head spins with all the noise.
In the end it's all worth it,
To witness the team I support win,
Or hide my disappointment if they lose.
No matter what, I will support them,
Through the good times and the bad times
I will always be by their sides,
To witness precious moments,
When they kick the ball through the goal posts,
Or witness the tragic moments,
When the bestest players leave.
I will always be around some place.
Dreaming that some time in the future,
The team I support will be the best.

Pauline Ada Hannah Knight

UNTITLED

The passion, the drama, the history,
The greatest and oldest of all.
The fat cats, the minnows, the mystery -
Most revered in all of football.

The world game in England - its place of birth,
When foreigners still all look up.
From 3rd round to final, all over the earth
They know it's the old FA Cup.

The final at Wembley, (most noble of grounds)
Is where now, we'd most like to be.
From 'White Horse' to dark horses, their memory abounds
As we all sing oh 'Abide with me'.

The 'Matthew's Final', the Lofthouse goal,
The screamer from 'King' Charlie George.
The big mistake, the starring role -
Within us, deep memories they forge.

Yes small time and big time, all enter the 'Hat.'
If you're down, you can start looking up.
And dream that it's your team that's first up the mat
To go lift the old FA Cup.

G J Hughes

HEREFORD UNITED, END OF AN ERA
(Dedicated to die hard fans who unlike myself go to every match still)

Through thick and thin, through rain and snow
On Saturday afternoon we'd go,
To find our spot in a windswept stand
A football programme in our hand.
We'd cheer the lads on with a roar,
And try to guess the final score.
We'd shared the glories of the past
And weren't to know it would not last.
That final year was not the same
We seemed to play a different game.
The better players simply went
To bigger clubs were money's spent.
We still turned up and cheered our side
And wore our Hereford shirts with pride.
And even when we faced the drop
Our enthusiasm would not stop.
That final match was very sad
For after all we didn't play bad.
Even the BBC were there
To record our anguish and despair.
Just one more goal would have done the trick
But the whistle left us feeling sick.
Is this the end of United's story?
No league status, no more glory?

Steve Harris

AN UNWHOLESOME NEW BALL GAME

It wasn't like watching Brazil
The tactics - route one, the score-line - nil-nil
The pies were too old
The Bovril was cold
I left in between 'The Old Bill'
But feet up in the corporate box
Watching what they do not know
Rovers? Rangers? Or White Sox
The contract's signed
So wined and dined they go
I remember stars in knickers
Nodding laced up leather balls
In black and white nostalgic flickers
The word Alzheimer's now appals
Nowadays shirts change with each season
Defrauding lads and dads of pounds
Supporters all must doubt their reason
Divorced from such expensive grounds
I write in anger more than sorrow
Without expletives for they're far too blue
That French World Cup seems like tomorrow
And yes, I can't get through.

John Wright

BLUEBIRD HEAVEN

It's hard to imagine
How it could be.
That historic occasion
On April 23.

It all begun
In the year of '27.
And ended at Wembley
In Bluebird heaven.

Thousands of Cardiffians
Young and old
Singing as one
So the legend is told.

This was in contrast -
To Arsenal Keeper Lewis
As his costly error
Meant that Arsenal blew it.

For as Ferguson closed in
The ball he did spill.
Cardiff City 1
Arsenal 0.

Cardiffians everywhere
Partying till dark.
Celebrating their heroes
From Ninian Park.

Wembley memories
Of the Beautiful game
Oh how I wish
For more of the same.

Martin Davis

SOCCER DREAM

As I sit and ponder on what might have been,
Having been to Wembley to see my beloved team,
Sitting and pondering as in a dream,
I think I remember the Queen,
Handing out the medals to my winning team,
Or was it just a dream.

Bill Walsh

WHITE HEART

I love you - dressed in silky white,
Your movements smooth and flowing,
On Saturdays and Wednesday nights
You set my young heart glowing.
And even then (for only then
Am I allowed to meet you),
I see you out with other men
Who constantly mistreat you.
A passion rises in my breast
Which sweeps away my reason,
One hour, and then a half, expressed
My feelings through each season.
Yet if I sigh, or shout out loud,
There's no way you can hear me,
To you, I'm one amongst a crowd,
I'll never have you near me.
But still, I'm not a lonely man,
I'm with you when I dream,
My Lily-whites, my Tottenham,
My Spurs, my football team!

Stephen Constable

OPTIMISM

The picture in my bedroom tells a merry little tale
All about two teddy bears and not about a whale
There seems to be a mention of an army black and white
And just a hint of fables and a mention of a knight
I have heard a lot of banter in connection with the 'toon'
And seen a lot of drinking particularly the 'broon'
Money cannot buy it and yes I think I'm barmy
The caption for posterity reads 'you and whose army?'

A quarter of a century has passed since I recall
A man to match our hero the legendary John Hall
He promised to reiterate the glory of those days
And eeh be gad he did it in many, many ways
We've had our little problems but they won't stop the toon
From basking in the glory of a match that's coming soon
Whoever gets the trophy will reminisce this way
And tell the bairns the story of the coming Wembley day.

I Chilvers

ALMOST A RELIGION

What is it about football
That makes the crowds roar
Could it be the cold damp feet
From standing on concrete floor
Or is it the excitement of a goal almost missed
Or is it the thought of after game
When they can all get . . . Drunk
It is a fallacy to think
The ref's eyesight is in dispute
And he really is looking that way
When a player is about to shoot
'Where were you ref didn't you see that'
Someone from the crowd
A player near the goal post
Speaking his thoughts out loud
But when it's all over
And ended in a draw
Perhaps the reason for both sides
Was the light was really poor
The snow and rain won't help much
And even less the fog
As the punters leave the ground
You'll hear words like, 'We was robbed'.

Jeff Jones

HAPPINESS TO TEARS IN 25 YEARS!

Remember when we were at St James' Park
We did so well in the unsegregated dark.
Followed by that great emotionally packed day,
When McDonald became quiet and had to pay.
The journey on the last train to London,
That left us vacant and hollow outside Upton
Great days we had when eventually voted in the league
Oh we did so well and did the business to succeed.
Chelsea, Millwall, Nottingham Forest and Wolverhampton
They came and suddenly we were bottom.
Great times we had in various FA Cup runs
So proud we have to remember to tell our sons.
Times changed and we were stuck in the same league
Those days meant we would never succeed.
One good season was promised, which we had,
The following season was vicious, cruel and sad.
It left us quite numb and forced us to sob,
Our memories went back to the original Hereford mad mob,
The FA Cup draw again, surprised us all,
We were going to meet Brighton, but this time we did not fall.
It was pleasing to see the lads on the telly,
And Neil Grayson score two goals with some welly.
Life began in the G M Vauxhall conference
We hoped we would be superior and show our difference.
Meeting many teams so tall and physical
Left us with results that made us feel ill.
With nearly 3,000 souls giving the support we need
Let's hope we have a football ground so we may succeed.
With a new chairman there now seems hope for HUFC
We'll gather on the terraces and wait and see!

Phil Tanswell, Herefordshire

I'LL STAND THE LOT OF YOU

'I'll stand the lot of you,' I said
to the other kids. They said 'Right!'

I was Wolves 1957-58:
Finlayson; Stuart, Harris; Slater, Wright, Flowers;
Deeley, Broadbent, Murray, Mason, Mullen.
The other kids were Rest of the World:
Banks; Pele, Best; Best, Pele, Pele;
Best, Pele, Charlton, Pele, Best.
Jimmy Murray kicked off for Wolves.

Wolves were well on top in the opening minutes,
then Rest of the World broke away and scored
seven lucky goals. Wolves were in trouble!
But then tragedy struck Rest of the World:
Pele had to go and do their homework!
They were soon followed by Best and Charlton.
it was Wolves versus Banks!
Now Wolves played like a man possessed.
Soon they were on level terms!
Seven-all, and only minutes to go,
when suddenly - sensation! Banks went off
to watch the Cup Final on television!
Seconds later, a pinpoint Mullen centre
found Peter Broadbent completely unmarked
in front of goal. What a chance!

He missed it,
and Wolves trooped sadly off towards their bike.

Martin Hall

THE GLORY ROAD

I wonder if they thought, those pioneers
who gave us football's jewel in the crown,
of all the drama, all the hopes and fears
the cup would bring in village and in town.

Teams in those early days were few and scattered,
Wembley was as yet a distant dream.
But then as now the only thing that mattered
was to see the trophy lifted by your team.

The FA Cup that breeds such deep emotion,
the ultimate - the greatest show on earth
where players strive with skill and deep devotion
to show the fans exactly what they're worth.

How do the mighty fall to small pretenders,
giants bite the dust and wonder how they fell.
Even the mighty Kop and Stretford Enders
have sometimes had to suffer untold hell.

The game has changed, with many other honours
but still the glamour of the cup prevails.
Those great twin towers that cast their spell upon us
will lure us on - the magic never fails.

J Handley

SATURDAY AFTER SATURDAY

Some years after hanging up my
football boots, a picture became

clearer as I viewed the modern game,
its players; and followed the patterns

of play. From *one up front,* to *four
four two;* back to the former line-up

of yesterday. Having seen Charlton,
Law and Best in the flesh, in open

play; John Charles, Blanchflower too!
It's fair to say I'm in favour of their

way: instinctive with flair. It's as
if I still hear crowds cheer and

applaud from the spot behind the goal;
rain, hail or snow . . . Saturday

after Saturday.

James Sherman

FOOTBALL FANS

Us football fans are a distinct breed,
It doesn't matter about colour
Or creed.

We support our team forever more,
Jump up, scream and shout
When they score.

All around the country we go,
Following the club when they're
High *and low!*

We stand on the terraces chanting
And singing,
Even more when they're winning.

Spending all our well earned money,
When it really isn't funny.

But one thing is for sure,
Next Saturday we will be back for more!

Sarah Grice

Match Day

Finding somewhere to park,
found our usual spot,
only half a mile to walk, saved a couple of quid.
See the usual faces
the loyalty says it all.

Smell the burgers
I'll have onions on mine.
That's our dinner sorted.
only half an hour to go.

Got our usual programme, they all seem
the same after a while.
The anticipation and the atmosphere
starts to build, the usual chants, the
only ones we know.

The roar, it's 3 o'clock.
Come on lads, easy ball, square ball,
all our shouts unheard.
Half time, that was quick.
The longest 15 minutes of our life.
Unscrew the flask, the coffee's warm,
the half-time results cheer us up.
Second half, the fastest 45 minutes
in your life.
Nothing's changed, the chant's the same
the ball goes into the crowd, nearly
touched it.
We get a corner, the roar suggests a
penalty, but nothing comes of it.

The final whistle blows, we always
stop to the end, you never know,
it once happened on our way out,
we heard an almighty roar.
They scored.

Never again.

Till next week.

J S Nowoslawski & Mark Nowoslawski

STOKE CITY

So Stoke lost the match
With Manchester Team!

They thought they were up to scratch
But that was not seen!

Peter Thorne was the bright spark
Everything else seemed dark!

Maybe the Britannia Stadium
Was not so good as it seemed!

It definitely wasn't old
But it was blinking cold!

At the top of the bank
That's were they sank!

From 1st Division
To 2nd Division!

Marie Barker